Marcus Dods

The Presently Controverted Opinions of Professor Marcus

Dods

On the Inspiration of Holy Scripture, Refuted

Marcus Dods

The Presently Controverted Opinions of Professor Marcus Dods
On the Inspiration of Holy Scripture, Refuted

ISBN/EAN: 9783337183295

Printed in Europe, USA, Canada, Australia, Japan

Cover: Foto ©Lupo / pixelio.de

More available books at **www.hansebooks.com**

THE

PRESENTLY CONTROVERTED OPINIONS

OF

Professor MARCUS DODS, D.D.,

ON

The Inspiration of Holy Scripture,

REFUTED

BY

THE REV. MARCUS DODS,

BELFORD, NORTHUMBERLAND,

IN

"Remarks on the Bible"

(PUBLISHED 1828).

THIRD THOUSAND.

EDINBURGH:
JAMES GEMMELL, 19 GEORGE IV. BRIDGE.
GLASGOW: AIRD & COGHILL, 263 ARGYLE STREET.

1890.

[*Extract from "ART AND LITERATURE" for May, 1890.*]

"Dr. Dods was born in 1834, at Belford, Northumberland, where his father was minister of the Presbyterian Church. The epitaph upon his father's tombstone, hidden away among Northumbrian hills, is still pointed to as 'one of the noblest in the English tongue,' and it is curious to notice that, in many points, Dr. Dods, with the instinct of heredity, seems to have lived again the life of his father. Professor Henry Drummond has drawn attention to this, and has remarked as also interesting, and still more prophetically significant, how this best of ministers (Dr. Dods's father) also lived

'TO ADVANCE AND DEFEND.'"

PREFATORY NOTE.

THE "Remarks on the Bible, in a Letter to the Corresponding Board, Edinburgh," by the Rev. Marcus Dods, were written at the time of the Controversy in Scotland and England in regard to a proposal, by certain members of the British and Foreign Bible Society, to publish the books called the Apocrypha, along with those of the Sacred Scriptures. Mr. Dods, in common with the Rev. Dr. Andrew Thomson, Edinburgh, and almost all the Ministers of Scotland, deprecated the circulation of Writings, held to be Uncanonical, in combination with those maintained to be Canonical.

The ground of opposition to the proposal was that the latter were written by Inspiration of God, but the former were not. The "Remarks" by Mr. Dods were published in vindication of the Inspiration, Infallible Truth, and Divine Authority of the Sacred Scriptures; and against the opinion that the Apocryphal Writings should be issued in connection with the Sacred Scriptures. Such portions of the "Remarks," as refer directly to the Doctrine of Inspiration are here republished, in the conviction that they are a full answer to, and refutation of the opinions set forth by Professor Dods, presently controverted, on the subject of Inspiration.

G. G. T.

"Welchen Leser ich wünsche? Den Unbefangensten, der mich, Sich und die Welt vergisst, und in dem Buche nur lebt."—GOETHE.

——◦——

"A *Canon* is just another word for a *Rule*, and a Canonical Book is a book that contains an authoritative *rule*, by which we are bound to regulate our principles, dispositions and conduct. A Canonical Book is a book to the dictates of which the most implicit deference is due, and from which we are on no account and at no time permitted to deviate. It is a book which every one of us is bound to read,—and to read, not for the purpose of sitting in judgment upon its contents,—of determining whether its precepts be right or wrong, whether its commands be reasonable or unreasonable, but for the simple purpose of ascertaining what these commands and precepts are, that we may regulate our conduct accordingly."

. . . .

" However opposite to all our views, therefore, any doctrine may be, yet if it be plainly stated in a Canonical Book, we are bound not only to admit it, but to cherish it as a sacred truth. However hateful to our habits and feelings any precept may appear; yet, if it be written there, we must adopt it as our rule, even though compliance should be painful as the pulling out of a right eye, or the cutting off of a right arm, and persevere till compliance become natural and easy. . . . If a Canonical Book were the work of man, it must be fallible, and therefore might lead us astray. The book therefore upon which we rely as an infallible rule, must have an infallible author,—that is God. And on the other hand, every inspired book,—every book of which God is the author, must be Canonical, that is, must contain an authoritative rule, to which we are bound to conform ourselves. For surely it must be obvious to every one, that what the Creator speaks must be binding upon—must be a rule to the creature." . . . .

"A Canonical Book is, therefore, a book the purity of which ought to be guarded with the most jealous scrupulosity. For if a book that professes to be Canonical, either omits what it ought to contain, or contains anything that is improper, it loses the character of a full and sufficient rule, and may lead those who rely upon it into the most fatal errors. Of this we have pregnant examples, both in ancient and modern times. The Sadducees adopted a defective Canon of Scripture, admitting only the Books of Moses, and thus they dismissed from their Creed some of the fundamental articles of religion, denying the resurrection of the dead, and the existence of angels and spirits. The Pharisees adopted a redundant Canon, adding to the Scriptures the traditions of the Elders, and thus buried religion under a load of super-stition, under which it lies oppressed among them to this day, 'making the commandment of God of none effect by their traditions.' "

"In our own times Socinians adopt a defective Canon, excluding from it the passages which record the miraculous conception of our Saviour, and thus deny the Divinity of Christ and the doctrine of Atonement." . . . .

"Is it then a matter of great difficulty to determine what books are Canonical? One would naturally think that it cannot. For, we might as well not have a rule at all, as not know what that rule is. In fact, we cannot pretend that we have a revelation from God, if we are unable to distinguish the books which contain that revelation from others, and are left in such a state of uncertainty that we may be easily led to adopt as the Word of God, that which in reality is only the word of man, or to reject as human, that which in reality is Divine."

"But can we suppose that our Heavenly Father has left us in such a state of uncertainty with regard to a question of such momentous and vital importance?—that He has mocked our hopes by professing to give to us 'glad tidings of great joy,' while He has left us ignorant where these tidings may be learned ? No. ' He has provided for us *all* things pertaining both to life and to godliness,' and cannot, without impiety, be charged with having left us unprovided upon a question of such unspeakable moment as this,—What is the Word of God ? And in point of fact, it is a question upon which men have probably never entertained a doubt, till they have adopted opinions which render an alteration of the Canon expedient. The Church of Rome, for example, does not teach the efficacy of prayers for the dead, because she found it taught in a Canonical Book ; but having first adopted the practice, she then Canonized the Book that teaches it. The Socinian does not deny the miraculous conception of our Lord, because he does not find it in the Canon ; but having first rejected that doctrine, he then tries to prove that the portions of Scripture which teach it are not Canonical."

. . . .

" What Books then are Canonical ?

" Holding, as I do, that a Canonical Book and an Inspired Book are one and the same, I have no occasion to enter either deeply or minutely into this question. The Apocrypha controversy has not yet brought any of the books of the New Testament into question, though how soon the principles openly avowed may extend their baneful influence to that portion of the Divine Word also, it is impossible to say. The defenders of the London Committee have, *as yet*, attacked only the Old Testament. In this I cannot but recognise the hand of a gracious Providence ; for to establish the Canonical authority of the books of the New Testament, requires a much more complicated mode of reasoning than is at all necessary, with regard to those of the Old Testament. There is at present no dispute with regard to the New Testament." . . . . . .

" Now, if it be admitted, as it is, that all the books of the New Testament are really the Word of God, then we are furnished with two arguments in support of the Canonical authority, and the Divine Inspiration of all the books of the Old Testament, so direct, so simple, and so resistless, that any attempt to convince a man who remains unconvinced by them, must be considered entirely hopeless."

" The first is, that our Saviour and His apostles habitually quote the Old Testament Scriptures, and appeal to them as to Divine Authority. When they could support their doctrines by a reference to the Old Testament, they felt that they had placed them on an immoveable foundation. These are the Scriptures of which our Lord declares that they ' Cannot be broken,' and for erring through ignorance of which the Sadducees were reproved. It is of these Scriptures that the Apostle Paul speaks when he saith ' Whatsoever things were written ' aforetime, were written for our learning, that we, through ' patience and comfort of the Scriptures, might have hope.' And it is of the same Scriptures that he affirmeth that they are ' *All* given by inspiration of God, and are profitable ' for doctrine, for reproof, for correction, for instruction in ' righteousness.' "

" If then we admit the Divine authority of our Saviour and His Apostles, that is, in other words, if we be Christians, we must admit also the Divine authority of the Jewish Scriptures, because their discourses abound with appeals to, and quotations from these Scriptures. And these Scriptures consisted then of exactly the same books which now constitute our Old Testament. That they had one book more, or one less, is not even pretended."

" The next argument is drawn from the testimony of the Jewish Church, a testimony which is quite decisive, as they are God's witnesses, selected by Himself for this very purpose. The great end for which they were chosen, was, that they might be made keepers and depositaries of the various revelations of God to man. The many promises and prophecies relating to the Messiah were not made at once, but at distant intervals, through a long series of ages. How soon and how completely would they all have been lost, had there been none whose duty it was to collect and to preserve them ! It was for this purpose that the Jews were chosen. This the Apostle Paul states to have been their *chief* distinction, that ' Unto them were committed the Oracles of God.' To an office of more awful responsibility men were never appointed. Were they then faithful to the trust reposed in them ? Or did they suffer some of these Oracles to perish, or did they adulterate them by mingling them with the devices of men? Their fidelity has never been disputed. They have often been ridiculed for the superstitious scrupulosity with which they preserved the Holy Oracles, for so far were they from admitting spurious books into their Canon, that they numbered even the *words* and *letters* of each book. For this trifling they have been laughed at ; but it sprung from a scrupulosity of fidelity to their trust, to which we are most deeply indebted, and for which we can never be too grateful. In many things that hapless people grievously erred, but the grand purpose for which God chose them, was fully accomplished. As witnesses for God,—as keepers of His Oracles, their fidelity is beyond all suspicion."

"Would that Christians could be brought to imitate them in this respect ! . . . . But unhappily a very different spirit prevails in the Christian world. There seems to be a dread lest the Scriptures should be treated with *too much* reverence ; and to prevent this, we are sedulously reminded that the Canon is merely a question of erudition, that it is no article of faith, no doctrine of revelation, no precept of Christ, but comes within the range of human opinion. In order to abate the too high veneration, which it seems Christians are apt to feel for the Word of God, these sentiments are inculcated, not by infidels, but by Christian Ministers,—have been published in London, Edinburgh, and other places, and by men who take a lead in the religious world—have been circulated throughout the length and breadth of the land."

"Now these cautionary remarks are intended to apply to the Old Testament, and are made by men who fully admit the New Testament. But if the New Testament be the Word of God, then these remarks cannot apply to the Jewish Scriptures. For we have in the former the most ample testimonies to the Divine authority of the latter. Let us admit that there may possibly be books in the Old Testament of which God is not the Author, and we must at the same time renounce the authority of the New. The question of the Canon, it is said, is a matter of human opinion. So is the existence of God, or the Divine origin of Christianity. But to a man who receives the New Testament as the Word of God, the question of the Canon, as that question applies to the Old Testament, is no longer a matter of opinion; for there is no doctrine more clearly taught in the former, than that the latter is the Word of God. In fine, we cannot doubt the Divine authority of any one book in the Old Testament, cannot suppose that it is either redundant or defective, without denying the authority of Christ and His apostles, and rejecting the evidence of those witnesses whom God Himself chose as the keepers of His Oracles, and on whose fidelity suspicion was never breathed."

"Upon whose testimony, then, are we to rely in this momentous matter? Upon that of the Jewish Church, sanctioned and confirmed by our Saviour and His Apostles? Or upon that of men who, though they are not only Christians, but some of them ministers,—men, an important part of whose duty it is to expound the Bible,—yet tell us that they have not yet determined the preliminary question, What is the Bible? And who have abundantly proved, that if it be a question of *erudition*, it is a question which will never be determined by them? There is no room for hesitation here. The inspiration of the New Testament is not disputed — and that being admitted, all the erudition necessary to settle the Canon of the Old, is just to receive in its plain and obvious meaning, what Christ and his apostles say upon the subject."

"The conclusion then to which we come upon this subject is—That *all* the books of the Old and New Testaments are Canonical, and that *no other* books possess that character. Upon what grounds does the Canonical character of the Apocrypha rest? Not on the testimony of the Jewish Church. The Jews never admitted these books into their Canon. This they would have held to be sacrilegious profanity, and justly so. Not on the authority of our Lord and His Apostles, who never appeal to them, and never quote them. Not on the practice of the early Christians, who carefully separated what was human from what was Divine. On none of these, but upon the authority of the Council of Trent, where, out of three propositions concerning the Apocryphal books, advanced in an assembly of forty Roman Catholic prelates, that which declared them Canonical had the greatest number of supporters, and was consequently adopted. This is the ground upon which the claim of the Apocrypha to be considered Canonical rests, and in instantly and unhesitatingly rejecting that claim, we are not only guilty of no error, but are performing a most sacred and important duty."

" I have said that every Canonical Book is also an inspired book. This I now proceed to prove, and without attempting to bring forward all the arguments which have been successfully employed on this subject, I hope to state enough to enable any plain Christian to assign a satisfactory reason for believing the Bible to be indeed the ' Word of God,' and an infallible guide."

" A revelation from God is essentially necessary to lead men to a knowledge of the truths that are connected with our salvation. The necessity of this is proved by the history of all ages. No nation, and no individual, can be named, who, without the aid of revelation, ever discovered the fundamental articles of religion, the existence of God, and the immortality of the soul. 'The world by wisdom knew not God.' Far less could men have ever discovered by their own unaided exertions the doctrines connected with the work of our redemption. Revelation then is necessary. But if revelation be necessary, then inspiration is also necessary, because an uninspired revelation is very nearly a contradiction in terms. As the sun can be seen only by his own light, so God can be known only from His own manifestation of Himself. If the Bible reveals the will of God, then it must also be inspired by God, since they who wrote it could learn His will from no other source than from His inspiration."

" The Bible contains many predictions of events which, to those who predicted them, were involved in all the darkness of a remote futurity. Many of these predictions have been fulfilled, and are fulfilling now. But the men who wrote these predictions could not by their own sagacity discover what was to happen many ages after their death. God alone knoweth the end from the beginning. When, therefore, we find that events which are taking place in the world *now*, were foretold by him who lived many ages ago, we are compelled to admit that these men were inspired by God."

" The Bible records many miracles. The men who wrought these miracles could derive their power of working them from God only. But the doctrines taught by a man to whom God gives the power of working miracles, must be true, for this plain reason, that we cannot for a moment suppose that God would stamp an imposture with the seal of His authority, or invest a man with the power of working miracles for the purpose of giving currency to doctrines that are either untrue, or of doubtful and partial accuracy. If a man work a miracle, we must listen to him as to God Himself, since it is plain that God has sent him, and speaks by him."

" The Bible contains the character of our Lord Jesus Christ, not professedly or graphically drawn, but exhibited in the simple narrative of a few of the leading events of His life. That character so exhibited stands alone. No being of a similar nature ever existed. That any individual writer, however unbounded his powers, even though possessed of that excursive imagination which ' first exhausted worlds and then ' imagined new,' should, from the stores of his own fancy, have drawn the idea of such a character, is hard to be believed, because no such creative power, nor anything forming even a near approach to it, has been exhibited by any writer, either ancient or modern. But that a number of independent writers, living in distant ages,—for the prophets may fairly be considered as Christ's biographers,—whose minds had never been polished by the discipline of science, and who were deeply prepossessed by Jewish prejudices, should all have combined to give the same view of the same extraordinary character, may be safely pronounced an impossibility upon any other supposition than that they were all inspired by the same spirit."

" That the apostles were inspired, is proved by the promises made to them by Christ. When He forewarned them that they would be brought before Magistrates on account of their doctrines, He at the same time desired them to give them-selves no anxiety about the matter, nor study what they should say. 'For it shall be given you in that same hour 'what ye shall speak, *for it is not ye that speak, but the Spirit* '*of your Father that speaketh in you*' (Matt. x. 19). Or, as the same promise is expressed in Mark, '*For it is not ye that speak,* '*but the Holy Ghost*' (chap. xii. 11). Now that this promise was fulfilled there can be no question. If any proof were necessary, we would find it in Paul's speeches, recorded in the Acts, especially in that before Felix, which made his judge to tremble at the thought of his own guilt; and in that before Agrippa, who was by him 'almost persuaded to be a Christian.' But if inspiration was granted to them, when defending themselves before Magistrates, that inspiration surely would not be withheld when it was much more necessary, when they were preparing those writings which were to be the rule and the guide of the Church, and of all believers in all ages. The promise was distinctly made to them in this case also. ' But the Comforter, which is the Holy Ghost, whom the ' Father will send in My name, *He shall teach you all things,* ' *and bring all things to your remembrance,* whatsoever I have ' said unto you ' (John xiv. 26). And again, ' When He, the ' Spirit of truth, is come, *He will guide you into all truth :* for ' He shall not speak of Himself, but whatsoever He shall hear ' that shall He speak, *and He will show you things to come*' (John xvi. 13). Here the promise of inspiration is distinctly made to the apostles. We are assured that this promise was fulfilled to the utmost extent. In all their writings the apostles speak of their own writings as the Word of God, and possessed of an authority, the rejection of which involved rebellion against Heaven. This they were not only authorised, but required to do, by our Lord's own declaration on different occasions ; ' He that receiveth *you* receiveth *Me ;* ' and he that receiveth Me, receiveth Him that sent Me ' (Matt. x. 40). And again, ' He that heareth *you* heareth *Me ;* ' and he that despiseth *you*, despiseth *Me ;* and he that ' despiseth Me, despiseth Him that sent Me ' (Luke x. 16).

c

Now, when such were to be the effect of receiving or rejecting the message of the apostles,—when, whatsoever they taught on earth was to be ratified in heaven—what they bound or loosed on earth was to be bound or loosed in heaven,—when to some they were to be a ' savour of death unto death, and ' to others a savour of life unto life ; ' they would have been unfaithful to their trust, had they not openly declared that their doctrines were not their own,—had they not most distinctly taught that the doctrines which were to produce such momentous results were not *their* doctrines, and most scrupulously avoided the guilt of mingling any devices of *their own* with what they had received from heaven."

" This guilt they did most scrupulously avoid,—this declaration that their doctrines were not their own, they did most sedulously make. Thus Paul saith, ' But I certify you, ' brethren, that the Gospel which was preached of me is not ' after man. For I neither received it of man, neither was I ' taught it, but by the revelation of Jesus Christ ' (Gal. i. 11). It is of the Gospel thus received that he saith, ' Though we, ' or an angel from heaven preach any other Gospel to you ' than that which we have preached unto you, let him be ' accursed ' (Gal. i. 8). Would the apostle have dared thus to speak of the Gospel, had he taught only his own doctrines? Would that zealous, but at the same time, humble apostle, who described himself as ' less than the least of all saints,' nay, as the chief of sinners, have ventured tó pronounce even an angel accursed, who should introduce any alteration into that Gospel which he preached, had he not at the same time been impressed with a deep and solemn conviction that every sentence of that Gospel was not *his* but *God's?* For if but *one* sentence of it was *his own*, that sentence might surely be altered, without subjecting the man, and much less the angel, who altered it, to so fearful a penalty. This argument seems quite decisive of the question. Our Lord promised inspiration to His apostles, when they were called upon to defend themselves before magistrates,—promised that the very *words* should be put into their mouths. Can we suppose it possible that they should be thus inspired when their own personal

safety was concerned, and yet not inspired at all, or inspired
in a lower degree, in a case where the spiritual safety of
believers in all ages is involved? No. In this case also
inspiration was promised, and they assure us in every varied
form of expression that the promise was fulfilled,—that they
spoke by inspiration. There is therefore no medium. We
must admit that they were inspired, or that they were
impostors."

"But then it will be asked, What is inspiration? What
authority does it confer upon the writers who professed it?
Upon this subject opinions have long prevailed, and are now
propagated with unwearied zeal, which appear to me to
render inspiration a mere name, and to make it a matter of
very little consequence whether a book be inspired or not."

"The common notion is, that the inspired writers were so
superintended by the Spirit of God, as to prevent them from
falling into any *material* error, and that in some instances
they had things revealed to them which they could not have
known except by revelation from God, but that in most
instances they were left to collect their knowledge from the
ordinary sources of information, to select and arrange their
materials, to digest their arguments, to gather their illustra-
tions from the resources of their own minds, and to clothe the
whole in language of their own choosing. It is said that
when they speak of things of a moral and religious nature,
they were so superintended as to be secured from error, but
that when they mention things of a civil or domestic nature,
there is no occasion to inquire whether they were inspired or
not,—that in this case, in fact, it would be hazardous to
maintain that they were. In order to save us from this
hazard, the country is at present deluged with writings, the
design of which is just to show us that inspiration is not so
very sacred a thing as we have been accustomed to think it,
and the effect of which is just to reduce the Holy Scriptures
to the level of other pious writings."

"That this view of inspiration reduces by far the greater
portion of the writings which we esteem to be divine, and call
the 'Word of God,' to a level with compositions merely

human, is perfectly plain. For surely I may, without in the
remotest degree exposing myself to the charge of arrogance,
claim, for the discourses which I am accustomed to address to
my people, all that those writers claim for the Bible.   In as
far as these discourses are of a moral or religious nature, I
certainly do hope, that in their composition I am so superintended by the Holy Spirit, and I would think it the highest
arrogance to attempt their composition without imploring
that superintendence, that they are free from any *material*
error.   And I may not only hope that they possibly may
prove, but enjoy the happiness of knowing that in several
instances they have proved efficacious, in the hand of a
gracious God, in recalling the sinner from the error of his
ways, and converting the soul to God.   The same thing may
be said of a thousand learned and holy books with which the
world has been enriched.   It may not only be said of them
that they are free from material errors, but it may be added,
that they contain the most luminous and forcible exposition
of the truth.   Are they then inspired ?   Yes.   According to
the modern and prevailing notion of inspiration, they are just
as much so as the Bible.   But would their authors claim such
a distinction for them ?   They would shudder at the idea.
Doddridge denied the plenary inspiration of Scripture.   He
held that low idea which his successors have so carefully
propagated.   Now, there are few men whose practical writings
have been more eminently useful than his.   Would he then
have maintained that his own writings were inspired ?   I
believe not.   Yet, had the question ever been forced upon his
attention, I am totally unable to discover upon what principle
he could have distinguished in this respect between his own
writings and those on which he has commented with such
ability.   He would probably have recoiled when he found
how exactly his notion of inspiration exemplified the adage
that extremes meet—that in lowering the standard of inspiration, in order to evade the objections of infidelity, he was just
plunging himself into the equally fatal error of Neology,
which, in order to lower our reverence for the Scriptures,
teaches that every book, by whomsoever written, is, as far as

it contains eternal truths, inspired. For whether we maintain, with the infidel, that there is no inspiration, or with the Neologian, that all books are inspired as far as they are true, the practical effect is precisely the same. The sole difference is, that the former goes more directly, the latter more insidiously, to the extinction of all reverence for the Scriptures."

"Again, if it be true that the inspiration of the Sacred writers extended only to matters of a moral and religious nature, it is obvious that there must be in their writings matters which are *not* of a moral or religious nature, that is, that while commissioned by the Holy Spirit to pen those divine truths which were to be the infallible guide of the Church in all generations, they were so little impressed with a sense of the awful responsibility of the office to which they were appointed, as to mingle these truths with matters of a personal, temporary, and trivial nature, with which we have nothing to do ; and then, without giving us the slightest taint (hint ?) of this interpolation of extraneous and irrelevant matter, they speak of that Gospel in terms as high as they could possibly use, had its every word and syllable been directly spoken by God Himself. It is of that Gospel of which the apostle thus speaks,—' Therefore, seeing we have this ministry, ' as we have received mercy, we faint not. But have renounced ' the hidden things of dishonesty, not walking in craftiness, nor ' handling the word of God deceitfully ; but by manifestation ' of the truth, commending ourselves to every man's conscience ' in the sight of God. But if our gospel be hid, it is hid to men ' that are lost : In whom the God of this world hath blinded ' the minds of them which believe not, that the light of the ' glorious gospel of Christ, who is the image of God, should ' shine unto them. For we preach not ourselves, but Christ ' Jesus the Lord : and ourselves your servants for Jesus' sake. ' For God, who commanded the light to shine out of darkness, ' hath shined in our hearts, to give the light of the knowledge ' of the glory of God, in the face of Jesus Christ. But we have ' this treasure in earthen vessels, that the excellency of the ' power may be of God, and not of us' (2 Cor. iv. 1-7). If this was spoken of the *preached* Gospel, surely it must

still more strongly apply to the *written* Gospel. But no.
Our modern apostles would have awakened the apostle
from his enthusiastic dream, and would have told him
that no doubt he and his fellows, when confining themselves
to ' matters of a religious and moral nature,' were divinely
inspired ; and farther, that ' we may rest assured that one
' property belongs to every inspired writing, namely, that it
' is free from error, that is, any material error ;' but he would
at the same time have reminded him, that to many parts of
the Scriptures, this lofty and awful language could not be,
with any justice applied, and therefore that he ought either
to moderate his style, or to limit its application. But as he
has done neither the one nor the other,—as he had no
modern Theologist at his elbow to lop away every luxuriancy
of expression, and bind him down to all the forms of logical
accuracy—I, who have never met with a guide in whom I
place greater confidence, must just believe that his language
with regard to the Scriptures, in the above, and in many other
similar passages, is both strictly correct, and universally
applicable. ' *Et si in hoc erro*,'—if in this I err, I will rather
err with Paul, than be instructed by the whole host of modern
Neologians, and their Calvinistic apologists."

" If it be true that the Scriptures are inspired only when
they treat on matters of religion and morality, then, in order
to determine what parts of them we are to consider as
inspired, we must first be perfectly instructed in religion and
morals. Instead of applying to the Bible in order to learn
morality and religion, we are, according to this principle, to
apply to them to determine what is the Bible. It then comes
to be a question, by whose views of religion and morals are
we to be guided, in separating what is Divine from what is
merely human in the Scriptures ? Every man will naturally
take his own, and the consequence will be, that every man
will have a Bible of his own, since that which appears rich in
religious instruction to one, appears perfectly barren to
another. Thus one man would retain in his Bible Paul's
medical advice to Timothy, and his memorandum about the
' cloak and books,' and Luke's notice of the name of the

island on which he was shipwrecked, because he finds in all these important religious instruction; while they who deny the plenary inspiration of Scripture would expunge them as things not of a religious nature. Every man would just place the stigma of reprobation upon every passage that displeased him, and dismiss it as not being of a religious nature."

"Nay, the same man would have a different Canon of Scripture at different times; because since the question,—'What is Scripture?' is to be determined by our views of morality and religion, our Bibles must be modified to suit any change that may take place in these views. Of the rapidity with which men sink into the most fatal errors, when they once begin to tamper with the Bible, we have many woeful proofs. Let us once admit that there are some parts of the Bible not inspired, and we at once become doubtful and uncertain with regard to the whole. Our reverence for it as the Word of God, and our dependence upon it, as a sure and infallible guide, are gone. If, to avoid the objections of the infidel, we throw away one text, upon what ground can we defend the rest? If we take away one stone out of this temple, however unimportant or superfluous it may appear to be, where is the dilapidation to stop? If one or two particular texts, such as those above referred to, were expunged from the Bible, perhaps we might not deeply feel the loss; but if the principle be once admitted, I see no limit that can be assigned to it, till it has shaken our faith in inspiration altogether, and launched us again on the wide ocean of uncertainty and doubt, without a compass and without a helm. Let it once be admitted that the sacred writers were not always inspired, and we need a new revelation from Heaven to tell us what part of the Bible we are to regard as the Word of God, and to read with all the reverence due from the creature to the Creator, and what parts of it we may safely set aside as only the word of fallible man. And they who are foremost to defend this view of inspiration, and to maintain that the sacred writers did not always speak by inspiration, have not been backward to show the extent of the mischief which it is calculated to produce; some of them rejecting not only verses and chapters, but whole *books*, as uninspired. And upon the very same principle, advocated as it is by orthodox and evangelical men, the infidel is fairly entitled to reject every book in the Bible."

"Let it not be supposed that I mean to attach blame to the men who first introduced into this country the low views of inspiration, which I am opposing, or to those who more recently defended them ; or to insinuate that they did not view the Holy Scriptures with the most profound reverence. They drew these views from a source from which they had long been accustomed to think that nothing but what was good and holy could come. The writings of the German Reformers were naturally read with great avidity in this country, when the Reformation took place here ; and the works of their successors, who had been bred in this school, continued to be received with the highest respect, after they had begun to decline considerably from the purity of better times. When these views were first broached, no bad consequences were apprehended from them. They were attended with one immediate and obvious advantage. They totally removed the ground of some of the objections of infidels, and were adopted as rendering the bulwarks of Christianity less liable to assault. The men who first adopted them had no design whatever to push them to any pernicious consequences, nor was it till very lately, that the fatal results to which they lead became manifest in this country. They embraced the present good, without having the slightest suspicion of the future mischief which might be fairly deduced from their principles."

"But that apology which not only fairly may, but in justice ought to be made for those who first adopted these views, is altogether unavailable for those who are at present pushing them to consequences, of which their early defenders never dreamed, and from which they would have recoiled with horror. For it surely cannot now be doubted or denied, that if lowering the standard of inspiration renders the Gospel less liable to the assaults of infidelity, it is only by leaving nothing which infidelity can wish to assail."

"The baneful consequences of entertaining low views of inspiration have been abundantly manifested on the Continent. The state of religion there, even according to the view of those who are least inclined to exaggerate, and who are best qualified to judge, is deplorable. From those cities and universities, from which the light of the Reformation shone forth to other lands, true Christianity has almost entirely departed. Where the light of the Gospel shone with the brightest splendour, there darkness covereth the land, and gross darkness the people. Floods of infidelity and Neology corrupt and poison that field, that once was richly watered by the living streams of divine truth. A vain foolish phantom, miscalled by the venerable name of philosophy, has usurped the place of the Gospel, which is now not unfrequently designated, even by those who profess to be its ministers, as the 'old superstition.'"

"Now, to what cause is this deplorable state of things to be attributed? Doubtless more causes than one have been at work, but it will be with one voice confessed that the principal cause, that which has had more influence than all others put together, is 'breaking down the barriers of inspiration.' And if breaking down these barriers on the Continent has produced such disastrous effects, upon what ground are we entitled to suppose that the same cause will not produce the same effects at home? If we transplant the bitter root of German Neology into our own land, will it not here produce the same fruit that it has produced there? And is this a result which any man can contemplate with unconcern? Would any man wish to see England become what Germany is? No. Every man will say that he would deprecate such a fatal consummation. But surely it cannot be denied that the low views of inspiration which have been imported from Germany, have long been producing Neology in this country, and are now producing it more rapidly than ever. The baneful consequences of these sentiments have made themselves sufficiently apparent even at home to put us on our guard. It has been remarked that not a few of the pupils of Doddridge embraced Socinian views. The same views were

said to have gained an alarming ascendancy a few years ago
in a Theological Academy in the South, where the same *theory*
of inspiration was taught.   It cannot be forgotten, that the
present Corypheus of Socinianism in England was formerly
theological tutor in an academy, established for the purpose
of instructing young men in views very remote from those of
Socinus.   Dr. Smith, the present theological tutor of Homer-
ton, maintains in his ' Scripture Testimony to the Messiah,'
that we have ' Scripture testimony for the inspiration of each
' and every of the books of the Old Testament.'   But the
same writer, when engaged in the defence of the London
Committee, has discovered that his former opinion was
altogether a mistake, and that there are several books of the
Old Testament whose inspiration is capable of no satisfactory
proof.   And here the Doctor is unquestionably right.   He,
and the others to whom I have just referred, have done
nothing more than merely carry out their views of inspiration
to their legitimate result; for, as is justly remarked by
Carson, in his able reply to Dr. Smith, to deny the inspiration
of Scripture altogether, would require the adoption of no new
principle, but merely to follow up more fully the principle
already adopted.   Nothing indeed appears clearer than that
if there be one book of the Old Testament uninspired, there
is not an inspired book in the whole collection."

"Nor are these the only monuments, portentous as they
are, of the fatal consequences of the low views of inspiration
which I have noticed.   We have unhappily an abundant
addition to make to these instances.   One most influential
member of the London Committee considers the Apocryphal
books as possessing a sort of half inspiration.   Another, a
very accomplished evangelical minister, and a very pretty
writer of novels, has been accustomed to expound the Scriptures for many years, but is yet quite uncertain what
Scripture is, and thinks that some of the Apocryphal books
may be inspired, and some of the books of the Old Testament
may not be inspired.   Others, described as men whose
eloquence and piety would give currency to whatever they were
pleased to assert, have been heard to maintain the deplorable

nonsense, that 'though the *doctrines* of Scripture are revealed,. 'the *Canon* of Scripture is not revealed.'" . . . .

"Now, while every means is employed with the most unwearied assiduity to unsettle the minds of the people on this most important matter, and to lessen their reverence for Holy Scripture, I conceive that it is every man's duty to resist the unhallowed attempt, and to do what he can to prevent England becoming what Germany, by precisely the same process, has become. Had I never had occasion to study the question of inspiration before, it would have been to me a very sufficient reason for rejecting the present prevailing doctrine on the subject, that that doctrine uncan-onizes no inconsiderable portion of Scripture, and lays a broad and firm foundation for that Neology which subverts Christi-anity altogether. And if they be the wise, the learned, and the good, by whom that doctrine is maintained, this just gives it a more mischievous efficacy, and renders resistance to it the more necessary." . . . .

"If the verbal inspiration of the Scriptures be, as a defender of the London Committee describes it, one of the wildest of all dogmas ; then I know of no effectual defence against that Neology which is at present propagated with such industry ; and of no remedy for that licentiousness of interpretation which is rapidly converting the Word of God from a plain path, and an infallible director, into an inextri-cable labyrinth, and an exhaustless mine of incurable doubts. The following considerations, however, induced me most cordially to adopt this ' wild dogma ' long before the Apocry-pha controversy existed, and that controversy assuredly has not lessened my estimate of its importance. By verbal inspiration I mean the suggestion not merely of ideas and sentiments, but of the words in which they are expressed. And that the sacred writers were so inspired, I believe for the following reasons :—

' "*First.* The usual way of conveying ideas to a man, is to convey to him the words which express these ideas. That no other method of conveying ideas is possible, I do not pretend to say. But while this is the usual and natural way

of communicating ideas, it is surely unreasonable to fly away
from this, in order to imagine some new and unheard of
method, by which God might possibly convey ideas to the
sacred writers, unless the objections against verbal inspiration
be of the most invincible character.   In whatever way God
might convey ideas to the sacred writers, they could convey
them to us only by means of words ; and if they were left to
clothe these ideas in language of their own, then we have no
security whatever that they have expressed themselves with
unerring accuracy.   For, ' How can a thought be known but
' by the words which express it ?   And how can we know
' that the words express the thoughts of the author, if they
' are not the words of the author ?   Had the inspired writers
' been left to themselves as to the choice of words in any part
' of their writings, they might have made a bad choice, and
' inadequately or erroneously represented the mind of the
' Spirit.'   *(Carson's Review.)*   Dr. Smith, even while writing
against the verbal inspiration, yet in reality admits it; for
he says—' It is an unnecessary supposition.   For the Divine
' influence on the mind of the inspired writer would as
' certainly guide the rational faculty of expression to the
' adoption of the best and most suitable terms and phrases,
' as if the words were dictated to a mere amanuensis.'   That
is, I suppose, that it is unnecessary to suppose that the
sacred writers were verbally inspired, just because they really
were so ; for if guiding them to the adoption of the best
and most suitable terms and phrases, be not just verbal
inspiration, I suspect it will require a clearer head than
either the Doctor or I possess, to show wherein they
differ."

"*Secondly.* It is admitted that in some cases verbal inspiration was absolutely necessary.   When the prophets, and they
who spoke with tongues, uttered language which they themselves did not understand, it is too obvious to be denied, that
in that case the very *words* must have been inspired.   Now,
it is very properly remarked by Carson, that this just affords
us a key to the nature of inspiration.   We are assured that
' *all* Scripture is inspired.'   If we inquire into the nature of

inspiration, we are assured that in many instances at least it was verbal. And as the Sacred writers give us no hint of different kinds of inspiration in those books, *all* of which they declare to be inspired, we must of necessity conclude either that all these books possess the same, that is, verbal inspiration, or that their writers have purposely misled us upon this subject."

" *Thirdly.* In proof of verbal inspiration, I may refer to the fact that an argument is sometimes founded on a single *word.* This argument is set in a very clear light by Mr. Haldane, in the Pamphlet already referred to. I quote his language,—' The uniform language of Jesus Christ and His " Apostles, respecting the whole of the Old Testament Scrip- ' tures, proves that, without exception, they are the Word of ' God. On what principle but that of the verbal inspiration of ' Scripture can we explain our Lord's Words, (John x. 35)—"The ' " Scripture cannot be broken!" Here the argument is founded ' upon one word " God," which, without verbal inspiration, might ' not have been used, and if used improperly, might have led to ' idolatry. The reply to the argument was obvious. The ' Psalmist uses the word in a sense that is not proper. But ' Jesus precluded this observation by affirming that " the Scrip- ' ture cannot be broken ;" that is, not a word of it can be altered. ' Could this be said if the choice of words had been left to the ' writer ? Here then we find our Lord laying down a principle ' which for ever sets the question at rest. The Apostles, in ' like manner, reason from the use of a particular word. Of ' this we have a example in Heb. ii. 8, where the interpretation ' of the passage referred to depends on the use of the word ' " all." Again, in Gal. iii. 16, a most important conclusion is ' drawn from the use of the word " seed," in the singular, and ' not in the plural number. A similar instance occurs in Heb. ' xii. 27, in the expression " once more," quoted from the ' prophet Haggai.'"

"This argument, even though there were not another to support it, I hold to be perfectly decisive. Yet even this has not escaped without an objection. It has been replied, that perhaps the Sacred writers did not use the very words

suggested to them, but other words having the same signifi-
cation, and this would afford the same ground for the
argument which is founded on a word,—that if the Psalmist
had used, instead of the word 'God,' in the passage above
quoted, another word having the same meaning, our Saviour's
argument founded upon it would have been precisely the
same. But on this I would observe, that it is a mere
gratuitous assumption, without any foundation in Scripture,
or any semblance of probability. It is not an idea that
would naturally suggest itself to anyone, but is just one
of those subtilties in which a pertinacious arguer will take
refuge when he is determined not to yield his point." . . .

"Either the *words* were suggested to the sacred writers, or
they were not. If they were not,—if only the ideas were
communicated in some way unconnected with the words
which express them, and the writers were left to choose their
own language, then how are we sure that the ideas have been
correctly expressed? For, to repeat Carson's remark, how
are we sure that the words express the ideas of the author, if
they be not the words of the author? On the other hand, if
the words *were* suggested, then the writers were verbally
inspired, and it is impossible to conceive any motive why
they should wish, or any principle upon which they would
dare, to exchange the words of God for others of their own
selecting. If they knew the words which God required them
to use, unquestionably they would use them. If they knew
not these words then we know not that the words which they
have used were equivalent to them. Besides, the notion of
the sacred writers using not divine words, but words synony-
mous to them, directly contradicts the Apostle Paul, who
says, 'Which things we speak, not' in the words which
'man's wisdom teacheth, but which the Holy Ghost teacheth'
(1 Cor. ii. 13). He does not say in words *equivalent* to those
which the Holy Ghost teacheth, but in the words themselves
which He teacheth."

"*Fourthly.* The verbal inspiration of the sacred writers
may be proved by this simple argument. Either they were
absolutely secured from any error in point of expression, or

·they were not. If they were not so secured, then they must
to a certainty have often erred, and their writings no longer
can be considered as the infallible standard of divine
truth,—a conclusion which some seem not unwilling to admit.
If we reject this conclusion, as I think every Christian will,
then we must maintain that they were secured against any
error of expression, that is, in other words, that they were
verbally inspired."

" *Fifth.* We may refer to the 'gift of tongues,' as a proof of
verbal inspiration. This was promised by our Saviour as one
of the *signs* which should accompany the preaching of the
Gospel ; and that the promise was amply fulfilled is abundantly showed in the subsequent parts of the New Testament.
When men were inspired for the purpose of enabling them to
preach to people whose language they had never learned, they
were surely *verbally* inspired. Yet, when they *wrote* to these
people, and to all the world, we are to suppose that a very
inferior degree of inspiration was afforded them ! " . . .

" And here again it is surely natural to ask, if the *preachers*
·of the Gospel were verbally inspired, and if that inspiration
was one of the appointed *signs* of the divinity of the Gospel,
is it so very foolish a thing to believe that the *writers* of the
Gospel possessed the same privilege, when it was so much
more necessary ? I cannot think so. At least, it is a folly
which I am not ashamed to avow, and of which I hope I shall
never be cured." . . . .

" I might with propriety close these arguments in support
·of verbal inspiration, by quoting testimonies from Scripture
itself upon the subject. But having already had occasion to
bring forward enough to decide the matter with any man
who will abide by the decision of Scripture, I consider it
unnecessary to enlarge their number. I shall therefore
·merely say, what, should it be called in question, can be without much difficulty substantiated, that there are few doctrines
more clearly taught by the Sacred writers, than their own
·verbal inspiration ; and that he who denies this doctrine, has
no right to find fault with the man who denies the divinity of

Jesus Christ, and the doctrine of atonement, since the same principle that justifies the one will justify the other."

"If the verbal inspiration of Scripture be not sufficiently established by the above arguments, I must consider every doctrine as doubtful and uncertain, since I know of no doctrine that rests upon more decisive evidence. And this conclusion will, I apprehend, appear still stronger, when we have taken a view of some of the objections by which it has been assailed."

"The first argument in defence of that low view of inspiration which I am opposing, and the *avowed* reason why that view has been adopted is, That it relieves us from a great many of the objections of the infidel, by cutting off at once the ground upon which these objections are founded. If we maintain the verbal inspiration, then the infidel may lay his hand on certain verses, for the introduction of which we may find it difficult to account. It is safer therefore to admit at once that the sacred writers were not always so guided and guarded in their writings, as to prevent them from introducing things which have no connection with the religious instruction of the world."

"Let us see then what advantage this gives us in dealing with the infidel. He lays his hand on a certain verse and says, Surely this cannot be inspired. I escape by saying, True, but then you see it is not of a religious or moral nature. His next question is, What are the parts of the Bible which are inspired? and how do you distinguish them from those parts which, not being religious, are not inspired? To answer this, I call in the aid of the learned, the wise, and the good, who have maintained this view. I seek in them for some general rule, some fixed and well established principle, by which I may separate what is human from what is Divine in the Bible. But my search is vain. I find no such rule or principle. On the contrary, it is obvious that no two men will answer it precisely in the same way. The only advantage then that I derive from this low view, is to enable the infidel to wedge me into a difficulty from which there is no possibility of escape."

"But even supposing this unanswerable question to be answered, I can derive no advantage from it. For the infidel lays his hand upon a verse which I acknowledge to be of a religious nature, and says, This is very oddly expressed. I must not say with the apostle, 'We speak not the words 'which man's wisdom teacheth, but which the Holy Ghost 'teacheth,' nor observe that it is nothing wonderful, if the wisdom of God should sometimes appear foolishness to man ; but I must say, The expression may be awkward ; I defend not the expression, but the sentiment. But should he reply, If the expression be a human and an ··wkward expression, how can you convince me that the .ntiment is not the same ? I confess I know not what I should say. And should he go on to observe, that as the sacred writers often assert their own inspiration—the inspiration of ALL Scripture, if we admit that in not a few instances they really were *not* inspired, we must of necessity conclude, that in point of fact they were *never* inspired, I know not how I could resist the conclusion."

"Such are the advantages to be derived from seeking to conciliate the infidel by concession—a principle which I regret to see creeping into some of our best Theological Treatises of late. If the Scriptures are spurned by the infidel, when they are presented to him as wholly the Word of God, it is preposterous to suppose that they will command his reverence when presented to him as partly the Word of God and partly that of man,—as 'a motley collection, composed 'partly under the inspiration of *suggestion*, partly under the 'inspiration of *elevation*, partly under the inspiration of 'superintendence, and partly under no inspiration at all!' Give the infidel one book, or one verse, and upon the same principle he has a right to demand the surrender of the whole Bible."

"But it may not be amiss to look at one or two of those texts which are supposed to afford the strongest handle to the infidel, and which some of the advocates of Christianity are willing to give up. One of these is, 'Drink no longer 'water, but use a little wine for thy stomach's sake and thine 'often infirmities' (1 Tim. v. 23). The objection to this is, that we cannot suppose that the Holy Spirit inspired Paul with peptic precepts for Timothy. But why should this be considered more strange than that God should direct Isaiah how to heal Hezekiah, or punish Asa for seeking to the physicians rather than to God? Besides, the text has a very obvious religious use. Without referring to the excellent moral lessons which have been drawn from it by Mr. Haldane, I may more shortly prove the religious use of the text thus :—The Faustinians and some other ancient heretics carried their notion of the unlawfulness of tasting wine so far as to pass the *cup* in the Eucharist." . . . .

"Another of the texts supposed to be indefensible is 2 Tim. iv. 13—'The cloak that I left at Troas with Carpus, 'when thou comest, bring with thee, and the books, but 'especially the parchments.' Surely, it is said, Paul needed no inspiration to write this, nor has it anything to do with religion. I consider the words, however, as those of the Holy Ghost, and whoever reads Bishop Bull's admirable sermon upon this text, or Mr. Haldane's comment upon it, will be convinced that it is pregnant with religious instruction, and altogether worthy of its Divine origin. Were I to preach in Rome, I would just take this text, and contrasting the affecting spectacle of 'such a one as Paul the aged,' after so many years spent in his Master's service, yet so poor as to make it necessary to send all the way to Troas for a winter garment, with the pomp, the luxury, and the idleness, which distinguish the ministers of Christ in that city now, I might hope to send some of them from the corruption of a court, to the study of their books and parchments."

"And if the disinterested and uncomplaining poverty of the great apostle forms a spectacle which can hardly be con-templated without profit, by one class of ministers, there is a still more numerous class that ought to study the lesson conveyed in the latter part of the verse. For if ever there was a time when it was necessary to inculcate the necessity of learning to a preacher of the Gospel,—to enforce the truth that, if possible, a minister should have books, and should read them too, that time is now. And surely we cannot read the verse under consideration, without feeling that this is a lesson which the Holy Spirit, through the medium of Paul's example, is powerfully inculcating upon us."

"Again, it is argued against the verbal inspiration of Scripture, that in many instances it was totally unnecessary. In the historical parts, for example, the writers could learn the facts which they have recorded, from the ordinary sources of personal observation, and authentic documents ; and consequently all the inspiration that they needed or possessed, was such a superintendence as to prevent them from inserting a material error. This mode of reasoning, however, l .ys grievous inattention to the nature and design of the l orical parts of Scripture. On this subject I have great p asure in again referring to Mr. Haldane's pamphlet. I s all only observe here, that we have the authority of the Apostle Paul for believing that they 'are written for our ' admonition,' that '_whatsoever_ things were written aforetime, ' were written for our learning.' It is necessary therefore that we should be assured not merely of their freedom from _material_ error, but of their absolute exemption from _all_ error."

"It is to be recollected also, that a very considerable portion of the historical part of the Old Testament is typical. Now, a type is just a particular form of prophecy. And if even the opponents of verbal inspiration are compelled to admit, that it was absolutely necessary in the prophetic parts, I think they must admit that it was no less necessary in the typical parts. For that any man should be able so to select, and arrangé, and state his facts, as to render his narrative a type and shadow of something future, without verbal inspiration, is just as obviously impossible, as that he should be able to utter predictions without it. For it may easily be shewed that the historian was as often ignorant of the typical application of his narrative, as the prophet was of the real import of his predictions."

"Another argument against the verbal inspiration of the Scriptures is drawn from the variety of style observable in them. There is hardly any species of composition, or any variety of style, of which the most striking specimens may not be extracted from the Bible. But it is alleged, that had all its writers been verbally inspired by the same spirit, they would all have written in the very same style. This argument appears at first sight to be really too ridiculous to deserve an answer; and it is with unfeigned regret that I must vindicate myself from the charge of utter trifling, in noticing it at all, by stating that it is one of the arguments relied on by two men, to whose superior powers I bow with the most profound deference,—Dr. Whitby, and Dr. Hill. An argument which such men thought worth stating, will be considered as of great consequence by millions. It must therefore be noticed, and a single observation is perfectly sufficient to demolish it. It is founded on a supposition, which I hope every man will reject, the moment that it is stated. The supposition is, that the Holy Spirit, who is the author of every man's wisdom and knowledge, cannot adapt the expression of that wisdom and knowledge, to every man's peculiar habits of thinking and modes of composition ; but has a style of His own which must characterise every writing inspired by Him— that He who giveth utterance, in all its varied modes, to all men, is Himself tied down to one unvaried monotony of style. Can anything be more preposterous,—I had almost said profane,—than such a supposition as this ?"

"But as this argument has not only received the sanction of great names, but is peculiarly adapted to the non-thinkers —a large class—a few farther remarks in reference to it may not be improper. There exists a great variety of tastes among men, and the Holy Spirit has graciously accommodated Himself to this variety,—I trust none will henceforth call in question His *ability* to do so,—by presenting the truth in a great variety of forms ; that if we be insensible to it in one form, it may attract us in another. The Word of God has often been compared to His works; and in many respects the comparison is just. When placed on some of those elevated positions which the Northern Metropolis affords, and contemplating the varied prospects that present themselves

in every direction to which the eye can turn :—while green
hills and mountains of dark heath, and fertile plains, pouring
their productions with profuse liberality into the hands or'
their cultivators, and 'the abundance of the seas, and the
'treasures hid in the sands,' and waving woods, and winding
streams, and naked rocks, pass in succession before us; and in
the midst of all, the 'crowded city' where industry plies its busy
task, and commerce collects and distributes the luxuries of
every different clime, and learning prosecutes its improving and
ennobling pursuits, it is hardly possible to avoid the reflection,
even if one could wish to avoid it, that all the various natural
objects which we see, are the work of the same great Creator,
and all tend, in one way or another, to the same great end, the
accommodation and convenience of man ; and that all the
men, whose ' busy haunts ' are before us, are employed, in one
way or another, in applying them to that purpose."

"The same remark is strictly applicable to the Sacred
Scriptures, where the Holy Ghost presents to us the truth in
an amazing variety of forms. But whether we be instructed
by the simple record of patriarchal ages, by the rites of a
typical worship, or by the history of a typical people ; whether
the harp, struck to every varied measure, now soothes the
troubled soul to peace, by the celebration of all that is attractive
in the Divine character, and all that is pleasing in His works,
or compassionate and merciful in His ways ; or swells upon
the ear in all the sublimity of the 'dark sayings' of the
prophets ; whether our attention be called to the unornamented
detail of that which no ornament can render more affecting,—
the life and sufferings and death of our Redeemer, to the
powerful reasonings, and fervid eloquence of one apostle, or to
the affectionate simplicity of another; still it is the same Divine
Instructor that teaches, the same heavenly truth that is taught.
In all the various forms which it assumes, still it proceeds
from the same source, and is directed to the same end ; for
'all these worketh that one and the self-same Spirit, dividing
' to every man severally as He will.' "

" And if, on surveying the scenes to which I have referred,
and which present all that can please the most fastidious

curiosity, and all that can gratify the most cultivated taste, and all that can most powerfully interest the man of business, the philanthropist and the philosopher, we might well be astonished, should we find a man so utterly bereft of taste and feeling, that while his eye ranges from beauty to splendour, and from splendour again to beauty, as it describes the circuit of scenes ever varied and ever pleasing, it meets no object on which it can rest with satisfaction; no sequestered retreat in which he might wish his hours of meditation to be spent, no active pursuit in which he might desire to be engaged: Even so may we wonder still more that there *are* men, and men too, destitute of neither taste nor feeling, who can find nothing to attract them in any of the varied forms which truth wears in Holy Scripture, where there are instructions so direct and so simple, that the most inattentive can hardly overlook, or the most ignorant misunderstand them, combined with a beauty that may please the most refined, and a sublimity that may delight the most magnificent imagination, —where, while the babe drinks 'the sincere milk of the word,' the loftiest intellect may gather ever new accessions to its powers, and the most exalted moral attainments may acquire that spirituality of principle and of character, without which 'their root is rottenness, and their blossom dust.'"

"The traveller in this delightful land, will often find his journey lead him through fertile fields, pouring forth their abundance on every side,—through a garden of the Lord, rich in the productions of heavenly fruits; and even in its most dry and barren parts, he will often meet, like the outworn and despairing traveller, (See Mungo Park's Travels, First Expedition, p. 244,) a moss flowering in the desert, which, by its indication of his Maker's presence, and his Maker's providence, will revive his exhausted energies, and renovate his forgone exertions, and nerve him anew for the prosecution of his journey, through what of the wilderness he may have yet to pass."

"Let us no more then ungratefully and ungraciously refer to the delightful variety of style in the Sacred Writers, as an objection to their plenary inspiration, nor build our doubts on that which is just a new proof of the goodness of God. Let us rather, as it well becometh us, in every varied style, celebrate that goodness which thus accommodates itself to the varied tastes, and feelings, and habits of His 'erring children, and recalleth us to safety and to life eternal, by the exhibition of His saving truths in every varied form."

"But instead of dwelling longer on particular objections, I may concentrate the force of the arguments which have led many wise and learned defenders of the Christian faith to abandon the plenary inspiration of the Sacred Scriptures, in a single proposition, to which a general, and, I think, decisive answer may be given. The proposition is this :—

"There are in the Sacred Scriptures many things which the writers very well knew without inspiration,—there are things which related only to their own personal concerns, but which are trifles to us,—there are things of which, in a religious point of view, we can see neither the meaning nor the use, and which perpetually expose them to the objections of the infidel. Rather than have them so, it is better at once to abandon the idea of their plenary inspiration, and only to maintain that they wrote under such a superintendence as to secure them from error."

"Now, the answer to this is, that the same mode of reasoning applied to any other of the works or ways of God, would at once be seen to be the very perfection of absurdity. When we look into the book of Nature, we see many things, not only so vast in their extent as to fill us with the most sublime emotions, but whose use is so obvious, that we cannot for a moment admit into our mind the idea of their destination (destruction ?), without shrinking at the consequences : let us just try to suppose that the sun were extinguished, and we shudder at the thought of the ruin and desolation that accompany the idea. But in the same book we see many things trifling,—things of which we can see no use, and from whose utter extinction we could anticipate no disaster. Nay, there are things that appear positively hurtful, and whose extinction would be hailed as a blessing. Are we, therefore, entitled, nay required, to conclude that these different and opposite classes of beings have not the same author? Or to maintain, that He who made all that is glorious and useful, did not also make all that is little, and—in our view—hurtful? Would such a mode of reasoning be allowed to be consistent with sober reason, or sound piety? Yet it is surely as consistent with both, to apply this reasoning to the works of God, as it is to apply it to the Word of God. It cannot without folly and impiety be applied to either. It is the very reasoning which, in former times, led some to adopt the wild dogma of two Creators, the one a benevolent being, who produced all that is good, the other a malignant being, who produced all that is evil. I had conceived that this dogma had been long exploded; and, with regard to the works of nature, I suppose it is so. But it seems that what is the wildest folly when applied to the *works* of God, is still sound good reasoning when applied to the *Word* of God. This is the *nineteenth* century too. And who, that sees what principles of reasoning pass current among men of common sense, can doubt that this is indeed the age of wonders?"

"There are things in the work of creation of which philosophy has not yet discovered the meaning or the use. Does philosophy, therefore, conclude that these things were not made by Him who made the sun to rule by day, and the moon to rule by night? She has been guilty of no such folly, but pursues her inquiries, in the hope that her labours shall be crowned with ever new discoveries. There are things in the sacred writings of which Theology has not yet taught us either the meaning or the use. Does Theology, therefore, conclude that these things were not spoken by Him who said, 'This is My beloved Son, in whom I am well 'pleased; hear ye Him?' No; but convinced that '*all* 'Scripture is given by inspiration of God,' she prosecutes her studies, assured that 'what she knows not now, she shall 'know hereafter.' Yet a class of Theologians has arisen, numerous and zealous, who would persuade us, that here Theology ought to turn her back on Philosophy and common sense, and reject from the Word of God everything of which she does not clearly understand the meaning or the use.

Difficulties in the study of the works of God never once raise
a doubt as to the *origin* of these works. Why should
difficulties in the study of His Word?" . . . .

" We may now then, I think, rest without hesitation in the
conclusion, that Scripture, *all* Scripture, is in very deed
literally and truly the WORD OF GOD ; and I cannot close this
part of my subject more appropriately than in the language
of Scott, the Commentator :—' What are they doing, who, as
' professed friends to Christianity, and holding the office of
' pastors, nay, rulers of the Christian Church, labour to
' persuade men that the books of Moses, and other parts of
' the Old Testament, are *genuine* and *authentic* indeed ; but
' speak so ambiguously on the point of their being divinely
' inspired, as to leave their readers in general to suppose that
' they do not believe them to be so, or that this is a matter of
' subordinate consequence ?' What would Scott have said
had he lived now ?" . . . .

" The truths of the Gospel are such, that they *can* rest on
no authority save that of God alone. He has been offended.
He is our judge, and He alone can tell, whether He will forgive
the sinner at all ; and on what terms, or through what
medium, He will grant that forgiveness. This privilege
belongs to every man. If we have offended a neighbour, he
alone can tell whether he will forgive the offence at all, and
upon what terms he will forgive it. He may insist upon
terms which we think unreasonable and foolish ; but still, if
we are resolved to be reconciled to him, we must just submit
to these terms. We have no right to dictate to him, because
we are the offending party. Neither can any other man tell
us what terms of reconciliation our neighbour will accept,
without his own authority."

" Now, surely a privilege which undoubtedly belongs to
ourselves when injured, does still more evidently belong to
God. I have offended God. Will He forgive me at all ? or in
what way will He do so? are questions of unspeakable moment.
Who can answer them ? No human—no created being. The
speculations, reasonings and conjectures, of the Fathers of the
first ages, or of their more learned sons of the last ages, amount

just to nothing. If we cannot, without his own authority, answer for a fellow-creature, much less can we answer for God. But when God Himself declares that He will pardon, I at once believe it: and when He declares that He will pardon only through the redemption which is in Christ Jesus, I am at once convinced of the necessity of seeking that pardon through Christ."

"Nor can it be any bar to my belief in, and acceptance of the atonement, that it may appear to me, as unhappily it does to many, to be an irrational and improper plan of reconciliation. It does appear to me to be 'full of wisdom, and perfect in beauty,'—to be absolutely necessary, in order to render the pardon of sin consistent either with the majesty of the divine government, or the sanctity of the divine law,— with the security of angels, or the safety of man. Angels desire to look into it, and they learn wisdom from it. The Christian finds delight, and comfort, and edification in meditating upon it. But even to him to whom it appears quite otherwise, I would say, You have no right to prescribe to God, nor to deny Him a privilege that you claim for yourself. If you wish to be reconciled to Him, you must just submit to His terms. These terms, instead of exhibiting a wisdom, and a richness of grace and goodness beyond all understanding, may appear to your narrow and limited view, to be unreasonable and improper. They may mortify your pride, but there is no help for it. God hath spoken, and nothing is left for you but submission to His will, whether you can see the propriety of what He wills or not. All that you have to do is to ascertain, from His own Word, what His will is. You cannot enter into the designs of, nor answer for a fellow-creature, without his express authority; much less can you enter into the designs of, and answer for the conduct of that God, whose very existence you could never have known without His own revelation. And if you never could have known even the existence of God, without His own revelation, how foolish is it to suppose that you can know His character, and His designs toward His fallen creatures from any other source! He who fancied that he could suggest improvements in the mechanical structure of the universe, had no power to carry his projected improvements into effect; and surely he would have been deemed worse than insane, had he refused to live in the world at all, because it was not framed in the fashion that he would have had it. In the same manner, you may think yourself capable of suggesting a better plan of redemption than that which God has appointed. But you have no power to effect the establishment of your own plan; and surely you must be worse than insane, if you refuse eternal life, just because you think it might possibly have been offered in a way that would have pleased you better."

"In short, there is but one authority in matters of faith, and that is supreme, and not to be resisted without guilt. All others, whether the sayings of ancient, or the speculations of modern writers, are of no authority, and cannot be received as such, without sin and danger. When my soul is in peril, I will not, and I cannot believe those doctrines, on the truth of which my hopes of salvation depend, upon any authority less than Divine. If God hath *not* proclaimed pardon to the guilty through the blood of Christ, then the speculations of no man, nor of any number of men, however wise and holy they may be, can afford me the slightest ground of hope. They may be wrong, and I, relying on them, may perish. But if God *hath* proclaimed pardon to the guilty, through the blood of Christ, then, believing this happy truth upon His testimony, I need not the testimony of any Fathers, whether ancient or modern, to give me a fuller assurance of faith; the authority of God is enough for me. I do but weaken, nay, degrade this authority, and shake instead of strengthening the grounds of my faith, when to the testimony of God, I find it necessary to add that of Fathers, Councils, Church Formularies, or my own reason."

"When the prodigal son returned to his father, he returned full of fears and apprehensions as to the reception that he might meet with. He felt that he could no longer hope for the privileges of a son; and he therefore determined that he would ask to be received only as a servant. Now, had any of his father's servants met him by the way, and assured him

that he would be received in the kindest possible manner,—
that his father would still treat him as a son, and load him with
all the expressions of parental affection, he would at once
have eagerly inquired, if the servant had heard his father say
so—if he spoke by his father's authority. If the servant
said that he did, then it is obvious that the son's fears and
apprehensions would give way to the most joyful hope. But
if the servant said that he spoke only from his general
knowledge of the father's benevolence, it is equally obvious,
that this mere opinion of the servant, would bring little or no
alleviation to the fears and apprehensions of the son. Nay,
had he, from the opinion of the servant, acquired such a
degree of assurance, as, on meeting his father, to express his
expectation of being restored to his former place in the
family, is there a reader of his history who would not have
been disgusted at his presumption ? "

"But, on the other hand, after the expressions and proofs
of kindness, with which his father met him—after his father's
embrace, and his tears—after the ring,—the robe—the fatted
calf,—if, I say, after all this, the son, still requiring farther con-
firmation of his father's kind feelings towards him, had gone
to question the servants, and to ascertain from their reports,
whether all this kindness was real or not; I would ask any
man of common feeling,—believer or infidel,—whether a
grosser insult could have been offered to his father ; or
whether his father would not have been shocked beyond
measure, to find that all his own expressions and proofs of
undiminished kindness, could not be depended upon, till
confirmed by a servant's authority."

"The application of this is so plain, that I need hardly
make it. I am that prodigal, returning to a father whom I
have deeply offended, and in whose house I feel that a
servant's place is all that I can venture to hope, and more
than I have any right to claim. A servant meets me, and
tells me that after a thousand sins and errors past, a father's
house and a father's heart are freely open to me still; and that
a father's yearnings have followed me through all my follies
and all my wanderings. This is indeed 'glad tidings of great

'joy.' But I ask what grounds he has for saying so, because
I feel that such tidings are too good and happy to be rashly
believed. If he tell me,—as, alas! Zion's mourner has been
often told,—that his report is founded on his knowledge of
my father's goodness, I can derive from it no hope. But if
he point to the written record of the Father's will, and produce
his own Divine authority, then I can rely upon it that I may
return to Him, with the assurance of being accepted. And
when I have returned, and have received all the manifesta-
tions of a Father's goodness,—when His love has been shed
abroad in my heart,—when His Spirit bears witness with my
spirit that I am His,—when my own experience testifies the
truth of His every promise, and the sufficiency of His grace,—
then I require not that the graciousness of His thoughts
towards me, should be confirmed by any inferior authority. I
rest not on Fathers or Councils, or on my own speculations with
regard to what God may or may not be expected to do, in
certain circumstances ; but resting on the written record, and
on the tried faithfulness of the Holy One, I say to them all,
'Now, I believe, not because of your saying, but because I
'have heard myself, and know that this is indeed the Christ
'the Saviour of the World.'"

"I shall be told perhaps, that this is not letter-writing, but
preaching. Be it so. Preaching is my profession, and I delight
in it. And much as I prize well conducted controversy, and
much as the world is indebted to it, I confess it gives me
pleasure to retire a while from the din of controversy, and
from the turmoil of battle, to refresh myself, and my readers
too I hope, with the fruits of that vineyard, for the possession
of which, I am called upon to contend." . . . .

"That error, with regard to the inspiration of the Scriptures,
which has proved so fatal on the continent,—to which the conduct of the London Committee has given such unhappy
encouragement, and which, in order to exculpate them, their
defenders are propagating at home, with such unwearied
assiduity ; was originally introduced as an useful truth, and
with the best intentions. Could they who first introduced it,
have foreseen the pernicious extent to which their principles

would be pushed by their successors, and the spiritual desolation which has been the result, who can doubt that the error
would have been at once abandoned? Even so, the good
intentions of the London Committee, can have no effect in
rendering their error less fatal. If any man think the error
trifling, he must, I should suppose, be one of those who consider every question with regard to the Bible—a trifle. If the
Bible be a trifle, and if the great fundamental principles of the
Reformation be a trifle,—if it be a trifle whether we do, or do not
know what the Word of God is,—if it be a trifle for evangelical
clergymen to preach, not merely that gospel which they were
ordained to preach, but also those Jewish fables which that
gospel warns them to avoid,—if it be a trifle to have our popu-
lation taught to view the 'Apocrypha in the same light as
they do the Bible,—in fine, if it be a trifle whether our young
men, who are training up to the ministry, be sent forth with
those low and loose views of inspiration, which they may at
pleasure push to results subversive of Christianity, or with
that reverence for the Divine Word, which will make them
anxious to have every part of their instructions founded upon
the 'Law and the testimony,'—if these be trifles, then shall I
also admit, that the error of the London Committee is a trifle,
for which it would but ill become them, as Christians or
gentlemen, to express any contrition." . . .   .

" The truth *must* prevail at last."

" Yes, Gentlemen, I look forward with confidence to the
final triumph of truth. But I will confess that I look forward to that day of triumph, through many an intervening
day of darkness, and through many a hard contested
conflict. We live on the eve of eventful times. I pretend not to prophecy; but it does appear to me, that
the elements of some mighty moral movement are gather-
ing around us with unexampled rapidity. And much
I fear that a desolating liberalism forms the leading and
preponderating element. And when I see men of common
sense, and of evangelical principles, putting forth such
Statements as that to which you have ventured to solicit the
attention of the world ;—when I see men celebrated for their

piety and their eloquence, instead of employing these gifts in
the support of all that is sacred, encouraging one another to
employ them in defending the most revolting heresies, by
means of the most deplorable absurdities ;—when I see
the liberalism of infidelity, and the meretricious phantom,
misnamed charity, of evangelical men, in ominous union,
directed towards the same object, I cannot think that I am
giving way to groundless fears, or unnecessary alarms, when I
say, that I consider the present period pregnant with dangers,
beyond aught that the Church has, for ages past, been
threatened with. I cannot but recollect that the witnesses of
God are to prophesy, 'clothed in sackcloth ;' and that before
the period of their final triumph, they are even to be slain.
And when I see men who have a high name, and occupy
commanding situations in the Church, busily engaged in
adding blackness to the hue, and coarseness to the texture, of
that sackcloth which the witnesses wear, I cannot but
anticipate that the death of these witnesses is drawing near.
Will it give you pleasure, Gentlemen, to be found at that
period, should you live so long, on the triumphant side ? Be
it mine to wear their sackcloth while they live, and to fall
with them when they are slain !" . . . .

" I regret to look back on the length of my discourse ; but
my text was the Bible,—a book from which many have learned
much more than I have done, but which few have had reason
to regard with a more profound veneration, or to cling to
with a more pertinacious grasp. Should my views of that
book be erroneous, they have, at least, neither been rashly
formed, nor lightly adopted on the authority of other men.
If I maintain them warmly, it is because I have won my way
to them painfully. My own experience abundantly proves
the correctness of the maxim,—' *Nihil tam certum, quam quod
ex dubio certum,*'—and it also abundantly testifies the power
of the Bible to afford the most effectual support, in that hour
when support is most urgently needed, and most difficult to
be found. Few have passed so far into the domain of death,
and been permitted to return. I have felt the breath leaving
me, that I expected not again to inhale. I have counted the

dull, heavy throb of my heart, as it grew fainter and fainter, fully anticipating at every pulsation, that it would 'heave but 'once more, and forever be still!' I have gazed on the faces of those dearest to me, till my eye grew dim in the blackness of death, and I could no longer see; and I have listened to the soothing voice of affection, till my ear grew torpid in the apathy of death, and I could no longer hear; and I have felt the icy chillness of death shooting through my veins, arresting the current of life in its course, till sensation itself forsook me, and I could no longer feel. And while thus placed on the very line that separates time from eternity, what was it that, under a deep consciousness of manifold guilt, enabled me to look forward in the momentary expectation of finally passing that line, calm and tranquil as I am now? Gentlemen, it was just that Bible of whose Divine inspiration I once as foolishly maintained the low view that prevails, as I thank God I have now long and cordially renounced it. I consider the opportunity afforded me, of bringing it to so severe a test, as one of the richest blessings of my life. And recalled as I have been to longer days, I wish to consider every day lost, which does not add to my knowledge of its contents, or deepen my experience of its value. I am well aware that the trying hour will return; and when it does, one of my most anxious wishes will be satisfied, if the prolongation of my life be made a means, however humble, of extending the knowledge of the Bible,—of maintaining its integrity, and preserving its purity."—(Pp. 8 to 103)

AIRD & COGHILL, GLASGOW.

www.ingramcontent.com/pod-product-compliance
Lightning Source LLC
Chambersburg PA
CBHW021440090426

42739CB00009B/1572